2015

D0286660

"*A Work in Progress*"
© *2014 Amanda Guerra*

Cover photo by Amanda Guerra

ISBN-13: 978-1512008227

ISBN-10: 1512008222

Printed in the United States of America.

ACKNOWLEDGMENTS

This book was written over the course of 12 years. From poems to short stories to essays, this book is a raw, somewhat intimate, detail of some of my life. I could not write this book without the people I have been blessed to know. Good, or bad, they have made me who I am, and I appreciate every single one of you.

I would like to also thank my good friend, Candice "Candi" Sanders, for taking the time out to help me edit this book. Yes, in a coffee shop. You have no idea how much you helped me, just by looking over a few things. Thank you.

I would like to thank my mother for always believing in me, and helping me select random topics for some of my fictional work. She also helped me get my work into the Library of Congress. Thank you, Mom. I love you! To my father, you kept on me to never give up, and believe in myself. If it weren't for your constant fathering abilities, I probably wouldn't be as driven as I am. Love you dad. Thank you.

To my siblings, you were around when I needed a listening ear, and someone to give an honest opinion. We come from a creative family, and it's fantastic! Remember. You too can do whatever your heart desires. A little cliché, I know. However, it is true. Thank you for being there for me.

Finally, to those who actually paid for this book – in any way, shape, or form. Thank you! It is you that have helped me make my life-long dream a reality. Remember my name. There are more books where this came from!

A Work in Progress

By: Amanda Guerra

Sometimes
4/26/99

Sometimes I sit here wondering,

Why am I here?

Sometimes I sit in my room wondering,

Why am I alive?

Sometimes I sit in the car wondering,

Why am I human?

Sometimes I sit in the classroom wondering,

Why aren't I dead?

Why isn't everyone dead?

Then, I know why I'm here.

It's life; I have to live it whether I like it or not.

Then, I think of family and friends.

Even if they aren't close to me.

My life is good; I like it.

Sometimes.

Monsters
6/8/99

I see myself in the woods,

I do not know why.

I see myself in the woods running,

Running from monsters.

The monsters don't understand me,

They think they know everything

They say they were teens and they know what it's like,

They say they understand.

They can't understand,

They've never lived the life I have.

They've never seen what I have seen,

They've never felt what I have felt.

They think they're wiser because they're older,

Just because they're older they think they know.

They understand,

Yeah right.

In reality they don't know,

They don't know what it's like.

Can you guess who these monsters are?

Can you understand?

My First Grade Love
6/12/99

My first love was named Danny,

We were in first grade.

He was my first kiss,

My first "true love"!

Then one day he broke my heart,

He was my first heart break.

I cried for the first time,

Over a boy!

He said he loved me,

Boy, was that a lie!

If he loved me he wouldn't have done what he did.

He was messing around behind my back,

He dumped me for her.

We remained friends,

Me, Danny, and her.

Danny still liked me,

He wanted to mess with me behind her back.

I said no,

She was my friend and I can't do that.

I'm not like that.

I guess I said no because I knew how it felt.

I left to move to Austin,

He gave me a hug and kiss.

He had a sad look on his face,

I guess he was sad to see me leave.

Well, now he knew what I felt like when he left me.

I guess it's true,

What goes around comes around.

He didn't realize what he had till it was gone,

Oh well, his loss!

The Man Outside My Window
6/12/99

I see a man outside my window,

Why is he standing there like so.

He's scary, creepy, weird,

Where did he go?

Someone's at the door,

Who's there?

Hello…

Should I open the door?

Should I look outside?

No, I'm too scared.

Is it the man outside my window?

I want to look, but I can't.

I'm so afraid,

I don't know what to do.

I'm answering the door,

Hello, anyone there?

Oh no, it's the man,

The man outside my window!

I'm scared, I freeze,

He attacks me.

I run, I'm trying,

I can't run!

Something is holding me back,

Someone is on top of me.

Help!

I'm screaming,

Can no one hear?

It's black,

I can't see.

It's so dark,

Help me.

Help me someone.

It's not dark anymore,

It's very bright.

What's going on?

What's this?

Blood!

My body,

That can't be.

I'm right here,

Unless...

6/22/99

Unless, I'm dead!

Oh no!

No, I can't be.

Well, maybe.

All I remember is pain,

Unbearable pain.

The pain felt like 1,000 killer bees attacking my face.

My head, my body,

How?

How could this happen and why?

Why me?

So many questions,

No answers.

Wait, I see him,

I know who he is, and I know why.

I guess I always did,

I just never realized it.

I know why I see him,

He's dead...

He killed himself!

My head has a gash,

His head has a hole.

He's talking to me,

How could he talk to me after what he did to me?

He's confessing,

He's telling me why.

He told me that he has always had a crush on me,

When I turned him down he went crazy.

He told me he watched every move I made,

When he found out I had a boyfriend he decided to kill me.

So, he did.

He came to my house with nothing,

He struggled.

Then when I screamed he hit my head against the wooden floor,

He hit my head so hard that I died.

Afterwards, he felt bad for what he did.

So, he got his gun from his car,

He kneeled by me and started sobbing tears.

Then, he said, "Please forgive me."

He shot himself!

He felt sorry for me,

So, he killed himself!

How could he kill me,

Then himself!

He was insane!

Wait a minute,

I hear the TV.

I'm not dead,

I was asleep!

Oh, thank god,

It was a dream.

Someone's at the door,

It's him!

It's the man outside my window,

It's the man in my dream!
That can't be it was only a dream,
Or was it....

Author's Insight:

I wrote this piece, randomly. It played like a movie, or dream. So vivid, and once I started, I could not stop. That seems to happen to me a lot. This may explain why there is more than one part. I just wrote as it came to me. Maybe I was watching too many scary movies.

The Day I will Die
6/22/99

I've always had a worst fear,

I guess everyone does.

But, my fear might be different,

My fear is death.

I'm always thinking of the day,

The day that I will die.

Will I die today or tomorrow?

If so, will I die of a gun shot, loss of breath, or even old age?

Will I die of loss of blood, in a ditch or in my sleep?

Will I die in the sea or on the beach?

*But, most of all I dread **when** I will die,*

Too young or not ready to die.

And when I do die,

What if I don't want to?

What if I die too young and never see what the future holds?

How will my family and friends feel?

How will I feel when the day comes?

How will I know?

I guess I have to sit here and wait.

Wait for the day,

The day I will die.

Tomorrow
6/24/99

Tomorrow comes and we take it for granted,

We never worry about tomorrow.

All we care about is yesterday or today.

We never look towards tomorrow,

We never worry about what will happen.

We could die tomorrow and we wouldn't ever care.

We will for a while, but then we forget.

We forget about it until someone else dies.

Why is that?

Why do we only care about tragedy?

How could we be so cruel?

How would you feel if you died and no one cared?

Tomorrow isn't that great, it's just another day.

I guess we have to make the best of tomorrow.

Look back on tomorrow and remember what happened.

You Think You're Better
6/24/99

So, you think you're better?

Well, I have news for you.

You're not!

Just because you have fancy clothes, cars, and money

doesn't mean anything,

You have problems too!

The more money you have the more problems you have,

You're so snobby and stuck up.

All you care about is yourself,

You make fun of other people just because they're different.

One of these days someone is going to come up to you and

kick the shit out of you!

Hell, you deserve it.

There are a lot of things I could say to you snobs, but I'll

leave that to people that don't like you.

That's a lot of insults.

Some people that you make fun of aren't going to take your

shit,

So, instead of getting mad they get even.

Take me for example,

I get even in any way I can!

Just as long as it's not murder...

You think you're better?

In reality, you're one of the lowest scums in the world!

You think you know everything?

Well, you don't.

When a person thinks they know everything or they're

better than someone else,

They really don't know anything at all and instead of being

better than everyone else,

They're worse.

You think you're better!?

Well, you suck and I hope one of these days someone makes

you realize you're not.

I only have one message for ya'll.

FUCK OFF!

Author's Insight:

Obviously, a piece written out of anger. I am, typically, a
nice person, but once I get mad, watch out. I believe this
was written because of the people around me. I was friends
with so many "types" of people in high school. It really
bothered me when someone looked down on someone else.
What sucked about this is, sometimes, it would be a
confrontation between two groups of people, and I often
felt like I was in the middle. Of course, I kept my cool, in

front of everyone. Me being mad, and having a fit, was not going to help anyone. Instead, I chose to take my anger out, privately, through writing. Not many people have seen this side of me… Until now.

Love
8/9/99

What is love?

What does it mean?

Is it sacred?

Is it not?

When people say it do they mean it?

Or is it just a word?

Is it special to some people?

Or do they say it to get something they want?

Do people mean love or is it just a game?

When it is a game,

Do they care about the other person's feelings?

Do they go after the person when they run away,

Or do they just let them go?

If they cared they'd apologize and run after you.

If not, their loss!

If so, will you take them back or let them suffer?

If you let them suffer,

Good for you; they deserve it!
If you take them back,
Remember what love means...

Love – *intense affection for another arising out of kinship*
or personal ties; a strong feeling of attraction resulting from
sexual desire; enthusiasm or fondness.

(Syn.) attachment, liking, cherish
(Ant.) loathing, dislike, detest

Author's Insight:
I've always been a hopeless romantic, though never
showing it as much, except in private or with people I was
really fond of. Like all teenagers, there was so much drama
around me, and my friends. The reason I chose to write this
was because I felt the message of love needed to be shared. I
could never really understand why so many people used the
word, "love", but never meant it.

Hatred
8/9/99

Why do people hate?

Do they hate because they have no love or they just don't
care?

Do they have no heart?

No parents to show them what love is?

Or are they just lonely?

Is it the past or present?

Was it something in their childhood?

What has happened or is happening to them that make
them hate?

Is it that their heart was broken and they want to make
everyone miserable?

If you know the answer to any of these questions, or if you
could explain why, tell me.

I want to know.

Author's Insight:

I also never understood how so many people could have so
much hate.

Cheating
11/6/99

How could people cheat?

They say they love you and will never leave you,

But then again they cheat on you with another person!

Yeah, that's love alright...

NOT!

When you go out or marry someone you're committed to them and only them,

Not their best friend, neighbor, a relative, or a complete stranger!

When you love someone you're supposed to say, "I love you", and mean it!

Love isn't just a word,

It's supposed to mean something!

When you "love" someone you don't cheat on them,

You love them!

When you cheat on someone it hurts them,

But, of course,

You don't care!

Obviously...

Because if you did,

You wouldn't cheat!

But don't worry,

You'll get yours!

You think you're the only person that can cheat?

HA!

Some day a person <u>you</u> "love" and will do anything for

might do the same to you!

Then they'll get theirs too,

Eventually.

It's like a big circle of cheating.

A damn circle that won't fucking end!

You cheat,

They cheat,

And so on!

Don't worry the people that commit adultery of any kind

will go to HELL!

It's a sin!

Hopefully, when they do go,

Their world would be crappy!

Who knows,

Maybe when they do go to HELL the devil will make them

imagine their exs are back for revenge!

I only have a few messages for the cheaters out there...

Eat shit!

Fuck off!

You're a bunch of BITCHES & ASSHOLES!

You suck!

Go to HELL!

You'll get yours...

You'll get yours!

I promise...

FUCKERS!

Cruelty
12/21/99

Why are people so cruel?

Is it because they have no morals or no rule?

Do they think they are mules and they could kick people in

the face?

Or do they think they're worthless & stab you in the back?

Whatever the reason is,

You shouldn't be cruel!

Do unto others what you want done to you.

Take the Columbine shooting for example,

People worry about what happened, who did it, and how

many people died.

But we really need to worry about <u>why</u> they did it.

My eyes
2/24/00

I close my eyes,

I see death.

Little people dancing around,

Laughing at me.

Make them stop,

Make it stop!
I open my eyes,
I see life.

People

2/24/00

People stare at me because I'm different.
Do I really scare you that much?
I stare at you because you're all the same.
It scares me.

Falling

2/24/00

I'm falling!
I'm falling into a pit,
A dark, creepy pit.
Where's the light?
Where did it go?
Help, help!
I'm falling!
Faster, faster,
Light!
Hey, you took my light!
Give it back!
It's mine, it's mine!

It's dark again…
I'm never getting out alive.

In Another Life
2/25/00

In another life,
I see myself in a size 2.
In another life,
I see myself as lucky.
In another life,
I see peace and harmony.
In another life,
I see myself as happy.
In another life,
I see a pure world.
In another life,
I see me.

Death
4/7/00

Death is something you don't expect,
Death is something you can't help.
Death stares you in the face every day, you just don't know
it.
Death is something that laughs at you chanting,

It chants, "HA! HA! HA! You don't know when you'll die.
I do, I do!"
Death, what is death?

In My Dreams
4/12/00

In my dreams I see you,
Why can't you be real?
In my dreams I see love,
Why can't it be for me?
In my dreams I see me,
Why can't I be yours?
In my dreams I see happiness,
Why can't it be mine?
In my dreams I see something I can't have,
You.

My Funeral
4/20/00

Don't cry for me,
I'm not dying.
I'll be fine,
Don't cry.
Why are you crying?

Stop it,

I'm ok I'm right here,

See.

Look,

I'm over here!

Don't cry,

I'm standing right next to you.

Can't you see?

Why can't you see me?

Why can't you hear?

Why can't you hear me talking?

I'm hugging you…

Hug back!

Wait a minute…

Why am I in a coffin?

Am I dead?

What's wrong with me?

I'm so pale…

I AM dead!

This is my funeral!

Author's Insight:

Many do not know this, except some family and people I went to school with, but, during my freshman year of high school (1998, 1999), I was "gothic". Even after 99, I often had some crazy thoughts that would take me to a dark place. For this piece, I thought, what must it feel like for someone who does not know they are dead? What must it feel like to have an out of body experience, or think you are having one, to find that you are, in fact, attending your own funeral?

Please forgive me
11/3/00

When I look at you I wonder,

What did I do?

What did I do to you?

How could I be so cruel?

Why was I such a bitch?

I'm sorry,

I'm sorry for the way I've treated you.

Please forgive me,

Will you ever forgive me?

I know I was wrong,

I know I broke your heart.

I know how it feels...

I never want to do that again.

I still want to be friends,

Please forgive me.

Author's Insight:

Written about an ex boyfriend. He knows who he is. At the time, although he loved me, I could not bring myself to love him back. Not the way he wanted me to. Not the way he needed, or deserved. I was going through a lot of issues, and did not feel worthy [he knows why]. Things got weird, and we ended up breaking it off for a day. We got back together, but it was never the same. We ended up just being friends, although, I know, it killed him inside. This is my apology to him.

When I Look At You
11/3/00

When I look at you,

I see me.

When I look at you,

I see us.

When I look at you,

I see us together.

When I look at you,

I see us together under the stars.

When I look at you,

I see us together under the stars forever.

Author's Insight:

Again, I'm a hopeless romantic. I often could not show it to others, unless they were related. So, I wrote about it. With the help of my cousin, we came up with this. ☺

The Other Woman

6/4/01

Look at her!

She's all over you.

Who is she?

I thought I was your wife,

You're supposed to be with me till death do us part.

She's so thin,

She's so young.

She looks 20,

You're 40!

Look at her legs,

They're so small and gorgeous.

Look at her face,

No wrinkles!

Look at her dress,

A red, spaghetti-strapped, bare-back thing, just above her knees.

She's kissing you,

Push her away!

Why are you kissing her back?

I know who she is now,

I've heard of her.

My friend told me,

She's the other woman.

Author's Insight:

When I was younger, I could make stuff up, on the spot. All I needed was a subject. One night, I asked my mom for help. I said, "Give me a topic". She replied, "The other woman". Not even five minutes later, this piece was done. Again something that came to me, vividly. This may explain some of the detail.

Why Does It Matter

8/2/01

I'm tired of people, who judge me for what I wear,

Why does it matter?

I'm tired of people, who judge me for how I look,

Why does it matter?

I'm tired of people, who think they are better than me

because they have money,

Why does it matter?

I'm tired of people, who think they are better because they

are popular,

Why does it matter?

Clothes, looks, money, fame,

Why does it matter?

If I Had Money

8/2/01

If I had money,

Would you like me more?

If I had money,

Would you go out with me?

If I had money,

Would you use me?

If I had money,

Would you tell me you loved me?

If I had money,

Would you come over more often?

If I had money,

ALL of you would like me more,

ALL of you would go out with me,

ALL of you would use me,

ALL of you would tell me you loved me,

ALL of you would show up at the door every day.

Dedicated To:

The Materialistic

Author's Insight [why does it matter, if I had money]:
I've had many different types of friends in my lifetime. In
high school, some of them disgusted me. I remember a couple
of friends wanted me to date a guy, because he had a car. I
felt sick to my stomach. Other times, the "fan girl" or "fan
boy" came out. Which I thought was not cool. I do not
consider anyone a celebrity. They are regular people, they
just happen to make their living differently. Yes, they may
have more money, but that does not mean anything.
Certainly, NOT a reason to date, or befriend, someone. At
least, not in my eyes.

You Thought You Could Fool Me

8/2/01

You thought you could fool me,

But, I knew.

You thought you had game,

It was so funny.

You thought I was blind,

Yet, your friend told me how you were.

You thought I didn't care,

I thought many times of playing you.

I'm not like that,

Why should I stoop that low?

You thought I was dumb,

Yet, you would never call.

When we were supposed to meet,

You hid!

You wanted to see,

To see what I looked like!

You thought you were "the man",

It was funny watching you make mistakes.

Watching you give me even more hints,

Hints of how you were.

You thought I didn't know,

You were wrong!

You thought you could fool me?

If You Were My Boyfriend
8/8/01

I know you've been hurt,
So have I.
But I know you're not like him,
Just like I'm not like her.
If you were my boyfriend,
I would make all your dreams come true.
If you were my boyfriend,
Nothing would come between us.
If you were my boyfriend,
I'd make you the happiest person alive.
If you were my boyfriend,
I would show you the world.
I would open your eyes to new experiences,
I would show you how much I cared.
If you were my boyfriend,
I would make sure everyone knew.
All I have to give is my love for you,
All I have to give is hope.
If only you could see how much you mean to me,
If only you were my boyfriend.

Haikus
8/16/01

The wind is still here
A leaf falls on an old bark
A feeling of death

A man sits puzzled
Wondering what to do now
Life is beautiful

The perfect angel
Her wings spread out like butter
Still she sits alone

The Day I Met Ashley
8/24/01

She was in seventh, I was in eighth. I had gym, she had gym. It was August 11, 1997 and her name was Ashley. She was pretty cool, I thought. She probably thought I was a dork. She probably still does. You see, I was "immature" and I would do a lot of stupid things. It took us a couple of days to actually talk. But, once we did, it was cool. You probably think I was in love with her, but I wasn't. She was just a new friend. I'm sure most of you were excited when you made a new friend. Or is that just me? She was cool and I liked being friends with her. Whether or not she liked being friends with me, you'd have to ask her. I even remember the gym uniforms we had to wear. They would probably be the same for the rest of the years the school will be there. They were green shorts and a gray t-shirt. They even had places for our names. The names were right in the middle of "Bedichek Bobcats". I looked forward to gym class. Not because it was gym, but because she was there. Every day I knew, once I walked in, my day would brighten up. We would always tell jokes and make each other laugh. We laughed so hard our stomachs and cheeks would start burning. That reminds me of one incident. I was running with Ashley and we were talking, me the most of course. Normally, when we talk and run our hair would get caught in our mouth. But this time, I swallowed a bug of some sort. It was funny. Well, to Ashley it was. I guess it was, too, although, it didn't taste very good. That class was great! I'm sure she would agree. Just ask her. Some of my best times, especially in middle school, were in that gym class. I'm glad I met Ashley, she's the best. We have a lot in common and we're both dorks. At least, I am.

November 10, 1998
9/5/01

I remember November 10, 1998.

I remember being so jittery I could jump out of the window.

I remember thinking today is the day.

I remember wondering, when will this gruesome day end?

I remember sauntering down the long, narrow hallway.

I remember finally reaching the double doors.

I remember leaping for joy when I saw my dad's car.

I remember convincing my dad to hurry up.

I remember reaching the hospital.

I remember my mom's pale, weak face, as she was disposed on her bed.

I remember when my little sister arrived into this world.

My Brothers
9/7/01

Sunday,

Cramping.

She went to

Schliterbahn the day before.

She woke up Aunt Irene. She kept telling her

She was tired, but she was not. When she

called the doctor she bled like a river,

They would've been sick. But not because of

Schliterbahn, They were dead two days before.

We found out they were boys, They would've been

seven. They told her they were in a shoe box, They never

got to see what the future had in store for them.

They never saw my brother, they never saw my dad,

they never saw my mom. They never met my Aunt,

my Grandma, my cousins, they never met my

family. They never saw my hazel eyes, they

never saw my radiant smile shining down on

them. This is what my mom told me, I wasn't there.

An Eerie Reality
9/13/01

Here we are getting ready to board the plane. What number is it? Number 11. Now I get to go home and see my family. OK here I am, seat number…12. I can't wait, I'm going home! We are taking off, why is everyone screaming? Why are these men yelling at me? Oh no! We are being hijacked! Hush little baby, don't cry. You are safe in my arms, we will get through this. Where are we going? New York! Why are we here? What are those men saying? The Trade Center! We are going to crash inside the Trade Center! I better call my mom. I need to tell her I'm not coming home. Don't cry little baby, go to sleep. When you wake up you won't feel a thing. You will be in a better place. You will be with the angels above, you will be with god. Shhhh…. Don't cry, go to sleep. When you wake up, you will see. You will see beautiful white clouds, and little babies. Little babies…like the one in seat 42. You will have wings when you wake up. You will be my little angel.

Author's Insight:

I wrote this after the events of 9/11/01, during a class. We were told to write a reflective piece. I chose to write in the point of view of someone on the plane. After this was written, I found out something similar happened on one of the planes. Children, seat numbers, etc. At least, that is what I heard at the time. To this day, I am unsure if I wrote something, while listening to the news, subconsciously, or if there was really something being channeled through me. Do your research and judge for yourself. Either way, I have been told this is a haunting and sad account of that day.

Word Accumulation
9/25/01

Water is good.

Water is pure and full of life.
It is good for you.

When I think of water I think of a good, wholesome, thirst
quenching liquid. Only it is crystal clear.
When you drink it is pure and without it you can't have
life. You will be reborn.

This liquid will provide you with purity.
Water will help in your rebirth.
This crystal clear substance can turn into a solid, liquid, or
gas.
Now that I think about it, I have a quenching thirst and
am ready to be reborn.

5 Line
9/25/01

Why doesn't she like what I like?
She thinks everything I like is stupid.
She's supposed to be my best friend.
She should know what I like, but she doesn't.
She's just my mom.

Mom
9/26/01

She is always there when I need her.
Sometimes she doesn't understand.
But, who does?
Mom is there to teach you how life is.
Mom helps you with your problems.
Mom is someone to talk to.
She is there throughout the tough times and the easy times.
You came from your mom.
She has gone through a lot to get you where you are.
Mom!
Isn't she great?

Author's Insight:

Just some, fun, writing exercises I thought I'd share. From the 5 line, came "mom".

People
9/26/01

People are hurting.
Do we care?
We only care for tragedy.
Why is that?
People are so cruel.

Things That Scare the Crap Out of Me
10/22/01

Dying young!
Roaches (especially the flying ones)
Stuff that crawls on me (little things/insects)
Being alone

Eavesdropping
9/27/01

*I just got in. I am so bored! I need to do something.
Man, that concert tonight was fun. I think I'm going to
leave. I know! I'll go to Karen's house. It's not that far,
I'll walk. First, I need to lock my door. Okay, which way
should I go? I guess I'll go down South First Street. It
would be pointless to go down William Cannon. Oh great,
the bus is unloading people! I wanted to walk alone, not
behind two preppy-looking girls. They'll probably think I'm
weird or something. As long as I don't talk to them I'll be
all right. These girls walk so slow. I think I'll just walk
behind them until they get out of my way. Maybe I'll ask
them to move. I'll wait for them to stop talking first.
Typical valley girls. Do they even care who is behind them?
Hey, their conversation sounds interesting. Her boyfriend
was with another girl! Like, oh my god! He probably
thought she was too slow for him; I know she is for me.
Jeez, please hurry up. He was at the concert too! Maybe I
saw him. I think I did see him! Who was he with? I
wonder. Maybe she'll describe the girl. Brown hair, hazel
eyes, about 5' 10". What was she wearing? All black!
Black pants and a Jim Morrison shirt! Wait a minute! I
remember him now. Blonde hair, blue eyes, 6'. I have to get*

out of here. Maybe she won't see me. But I didn't know he was her boyfriend. Why did I kiss him? Why am I feeling guilty? I didn't know. If I had known I wouldn't have done it. But... I didn't know. I'm ok. I didn't know! Oh no, I said that out loud! She heard me. Oh s#@*! Who's that? They're pulling over. It's him. It's her boyfriend. He didn't stop in front of her; he stopped in front of me. Oh good! I don't need to walk, I have a ride.

Author's Insight (from 10/3/01):

When I wrote this story I didn't really know the purpose of it. I just sat down and started writing (as usual). My mom just told me to write about someone cheating. She gave me a subject and I went on from there. The characters in my story are just everyday people. I thought it would be interesting to make a conflict between preps & a grungy-looking person. After all, these people have conflicts every day. I thought it would entertain the reader. It would be funny if a "stereotypical prep" and a "stereotypical banger" had a conflict [over] a guy. [It is funny to see that the less fortunate girl, leaves with the guy].

The Journey
9/27/01

I'm walking, but I don't know where. I think I was going to my cousin's house. I wanted to see if she wanted to go to the movies with me. All of a sudden, I saw this beautiful, shiny, extraordinary rock. It was not a regular rock though. It was the kind of rock that you didn't want to see lying on the road. It didn't deserve to be outcast all by itself. It deserved to be in the spotlight. When the spotlight was on this rock it stole the show. I'm serious. It got me thinking. It got me thinking of this bright, shiny rock on stage with a bunch of different rocks. Just imagine a rock on the stage with its fellow rocks busting a move right in front of everyone. The little rock with a guitar and a little, teeny weeny, mic. Man, that's going to be a famous rock! Then, I spot someone coming down the street. I don't know who he is. But, he sure was hot. Blonde hair, blue eyes, 6'. Man, what a hotty! So, I came up with a stupid idea. I decided to tell him about the rock. He acted like he was really interested. Then, I started telling him about the rock and its teeny weeny microphone. BUZZ.... Well, there goes my alarm. Why did I dream about a rock? My mom is calling me downstairs. Apparently, her friend has a little boy that just moved to

Austin with his dad. He just happened to be my age. How ironic! It seems we have a date to go to a rock concert Saturday night.

Author's Insight (from 10/3/01):
When I wrote this story I thought it would be funny to write about a rock. After all, people don't normally write about rocks. I think it is cool how I try to describe something special and then I end up describing a rock. The [guy] I saw was also in another one of my stories. I thought it would be interesting to put him in this story. This story, I thought, would be a good way to show how this boy and girl meet. [Tells of a dream sequence that later comes true. It also tells what the rock, in her dream, symbolizes]

The Gift
9/28/01

Why does this always have to happen to me? I always have something horrible happen to me! My test was positive! Why? I don't see how. How could I get cancer? It doesn't run in my family. I'm never out in the sun. How? Damn it! Now, I'm going to be known throughout my neighborhood as "John the Cancer Patient!" Look at this! I think my hair is falling out! I'm only 23 and I'm going bald! I need some fresh air. I can't bear to look myself in the mirror again. Oh look. It's Sarah! The little child, that everyone loves. She's coming my way! Maybe she'll call me "John the Cancer Patient!" I guess she wants to talk to me. "Why are you so sad?" Gee, I wonder. She just made me feel a lot better. Why is she looking at me like that? "You're sick." No, really. A hug! She gave me a hug! There she goes, skipping away. What a sweet little girl. What am I saying? I'm angry! I shouldn't be angry. I'm not the only one that has cancer. There are other people out there. I'm a nice person. I just need to keep my head straight. I am ok. I need to go back inside. I need to set myself straight. I'll look in the mirror one more time. Hey, I'm not that bad, I'm just my own self. I'm fine. I'll live. Carpe Diem.

These are the events that happened to me 10 years ago. I've been cancer free ever since. Now, let's hear your story. After all, this is a place for cancer survivors.

Author's Insight:

Written as an interior monologue. When I wrote this, I thought what must it be like? To be healthy one minute, and diagnosed the next. My first thought was anger. I have another version of this later. You can decide which one you like better, if you like them at all.

Dedication
10/10/01

Dedicated To:

All Who Have Died

A tear is shed every time we hear of a death.

This world is so hectic. People killing, people dying. Why must life be so tragic? Why do we only care about the bad? Why not the good? The media today shows visions of violence and death. Why not peace and quiet? Hate has swallowed us up like a whale does a fish. In this world we are small. We could all work together to be strong. There is plenty of room to show love, plenty of room to show peace, plenty of room to show happiness. But, these terrorists have conquered us with hate. Why can't we overcome this demon, this hatred, these cowards? Why must we fall on our knees and beg for peace? Why not talk and listen? Instead of war, we should rebuild. Children are dying, people are crying. Why must our generation live like this?

They say history repeats itself. Why? Instead of repeating what has been done, we should start a new beginning, a new beginning as one.

A single rose is all we can give.
A petal for each death.

A Creepy, Made Up Story
11/11/01

Amanda knew there was something wrong with the house. She couldn't put her finger on it but something was really bugging her. Something about the freshly-painted house was eerie. Even though she had new carpet and her own room, she couldn't bear to be alone. When her parents left her by herself she wouldn't go upstairs. Even if her brother or sister were with her she couldn't bring herself to climb the spiral staircase, especially, at night. She just couldn't walk down that long, dark, narrow hallway without her back getting cold or her hairs standing up. Sometimes when she would hear noises at night she would tell herself, "It's only your imagination. You're too old to be afraid." For some reason, every time she would say that her room would get really cold and her breath would look like dry ice.

One day, Amanda and her brother were at home when they heard a door slam. They figured it was the wind. After all, the a/c wasn't working and they had the windows open. That night, as Amanda took a shower, she noticed that the water kept getting hotter and hotter. It felt like hot coals burning through her flesh. She could see her skin turning blood red. She tried turning off the shower but nothing worked. As she struggled with the scorching metal knobs she heard someone say her name. She thought it was her brother and asked for help. When she lifted the curtain to find her brother, no one was there. She looked and saw, on the fog-filled mirror, a sentence. She didn't know what it meant but it sent chills down her spine. She started yelling for her mom. Just as her mom opened the door, the water turned cold and the message disappeared. Her skin was back to normal as well. Her mom thought she was crazy and seeing things.

The next morning she woke up to go to school. For some reason she got really nauseous. As she sprinted down the hall toward the bathroom she heard someone humming. As she turned around, to look toward her room, she saw a young man sitting on her bed staring at her stomach. She blinked and he was gone. All of a sudden, she dropped to her knees, grabbing her stomach. She was in excruciating pain. It felt like 1,000 needles stabbing her in her ovaries. Out of nowhere, she felt a cold breeze and began to rise. While she was rising, she noticed a bright, white light. When she woke up she noticed she was on her bed. Her mom was on the phone calling her in. She could not hear what her mom was saying. But as she listened, in a faint voice, her mom said, "I think she's pregnant." This was funny to Amanda because she was a virgin. When she was done her mom left, thinking she was asleep. Amanda turned her head in terror as she noticed a white male holding her hand. She noticed he had blonde hair and blue eyes. He looked about 6' and was in his early twenties. Her dad and brother were not home. So, she knew it was not them. As she began to think, she noticed he looked familiar but she didn't know from where. Suddenly, she started cramping and dozed off. But, before she went to sleep she opened her eyes and noticed the man was gone. She finally realized who he was. It was the man she saw humming on her bed! That whole day, as she lay in bed, she thought of that man and how cute he was. However, for the rest of that night she did not see him.

A week went by and she hadn't seen him. She began to feel like he wasn't coming back. She thought her friend was gone. That night, when Amanda got out of the shower, she saw the message on the mirror. This time she knew who wrote it and she understood. As she went into her room she felt a cold breeze. She knew who it was and closed the door behind her. From that night on, for about a month, Amanda would see the message on the mirror, go to her room, and close the door. Every now and then her mom would hear noises in Amanda's room. But when she opened the door, Amanda would be asleep. Then, her mom would go back to bed and hear the noises again. She didn't know what it was, but she was frightened for Amanda. She knew someone or something was trying to hurt her. She could not do anything for her daughter. She couldn't see or hear what was going on in her daughter's room. One night, in her room, Amanda noticed another message on her mirror. It was different! The message she saw in the bathroom before read, "I want you." This one read, "You will be mine." For some strange reason, she thought she understood the messages. Two weeks went by and it was now Amanda's birthday. She figured her friend was gone. After her party she went into her room and invited her friend back in. BIG mistake! As she called out his name, slowly a message was written on her mirror. It read, "I will have you tonight." Suddenly, the door slammed. She tried to move but she couldn't. It was as though someone was on top of her, holding her against her will. Then, her friend showed up. But this time he was on top of her. He began pushing her hands down on her bed. Something was keeping her from screaming. She could not figure out what it was. She must have been too afraid to scream. She struggled with her "friend" and finally let out a big yell. Shortly after, her parents ran up the stairs. They started banging on the door but it was locked. This was odd because there was no lock on the door. Amanda hollered, "Why are you doing this!" as she looked through John's eyes, he pointed at her computer.

As she looked over, the computer turned on and she noticed a document. It was a scary story she wrote her senior year! She began screeching and struggling to get up. No matter what she did he pushed down harder and harder on her and became more and more angry. She began to yell, "Stop it! You're hurting me!" As she said this, John had a big smirk on his face. Her parents were outside listening in horror as their daughter let out her final cry for help. Just then her parents broke down the door and found the bed drenched in water. As they looked for their daughter, they noticed smoke coming from the bathroom, as if the hot water was on. As they entered the bathroom, they noticed the curtain was hot and the water was off. They opened the curtain, in hopes their daughter was there. But, when they opened it, no one was there. They turned to see a message on the mirror that read, "I finally have her!" Underneath, "HELP ME!" was written in their daughter's handwriting.

They never could figure out what happened to their daughter's body or where the smoke was coming from. The locals say her story simply came true. Others say her friend came for her that night and she was doomed to be his lover forever. After all, she was going to bear his child.

Unfortunately, one year later, Amanda's mom died of mysterious circumstances.

Some say when you pass by the house at night you can still hear the cries of Amanda as she struggles to get out of her room. Some say they hear banging on her door, as if someone is trying to help her. Everyone who visits notices a woman, dressed in black, roaming the upstairs hallway. They say it is Amanda's mom still searching. Searching, for her daughter's body.

Author's Insight:

When we moved in to our latest place (my sophomore year of high school), I kept getting creeped out. As soon as I walked in, something was off. I didn't pay too much attention, until I picked my room (yes, I picked it). When I had a bed in my room, I rarely slept in there. When my computer was in my room, I kept getting chills down my spine. To this day, I rarely go into my room. If I do, I always make note of how long I am in there, and what I am doing. It is a strange feeling. Add that with some things I have seen, and felt, in the past. Well, you get it. Anyway, in true form, I wrote this creepy story (my senior year of high school). Why? Just to add to the creepiness. Plus, it's always nice to see everyone's reaction, once they finally read it. :-o

It is about four in the morning, and as I sit here, typing this, I have succeeded, yet again, in creeping myself out...

Terrorism Strikes Again
Japan learned years ago...

Dear Terrorists,

I hope you are happy for bringing us together. I hope you are happy for reuniting America. I hope you are happy for not bringing us down, but for making us stronger. Instead of you making us individuals, you have made us a unit. Looks like your "carefully" planned attack backfired. Too bad you are not alive to see it. You have taken lives, as well as your own, in the drastically, cowardly act of hatred. I don't understand why you hate us so much. What did we do to you? What did innocent people, innocent lives, innocent families have to do with your hatred? You have made children, innocent children, orphans. You have made us mourn. But, not for long. Japan learned years ago what happens when you mess with our country. Japan learned what happens when you take the lives of the innocent. Japan also learned how powerful we can all be when you interfere with our lives. Japan learned, you can't bring us down. You can only make us more powerful, more compassionate, and more religious. You have no idea how our power will make us come together. You have no idea how much trouble you have caused. Too bad you are not alive to learn how we will retaliate against your cowardly actions. But, you will soon find out.

Sincerely,
Amanda M. Guerra

Author's Insight:
Written as an, angry, editorial/news letter to the terrorists of 9/11. I do not remember what day I wrote this, however. I know it was from 2001.

My Head Injury
(A.K.A. Why I am the way I am)
1/20/02

All I remember was my cousin and I jumping on the bed, like monkeys. We were a couple of kids. I was six, she was five. She was trying to scare me. Unfortunately, it worked. I remember stepping back from my bed to get away. All of a sudden, I fell! I thought I would just fall on the floor, cry and that would be it. Little did I know, right behind me, there was an old wooden desk with sharp points at the corners. I tried turning my head to check if there was anything behind me. As I turned, I hit the left side of my head on one of the corners. It felt like someone stabbed me in the brain. The pain was unbearable. I remember lying on the floor. Everything was blurry! It went black after a while. When I opened my eyes, my cousin was sitting on the bed crying.

She was saying, "I'm sorry, I'm sorry! I didn't mean to!"

Then I looked at my mom, dazed, and she was crying. She told my cousin to tell her dad we're going to the hospital.

Then, I remember my mom saying, "She has a gash, she has a gash!" Then, I remember her saying, "I see blood!"

As I was lying there, I turned my head towards the right and noticed my dad in the kitchen. He was upset because I didn't listen to him.

I looked up at my mom and she was hysterical. I felt something lift me up. It was my dad! He was carrying me (bridal style). He put me in the car. I had to tilt my head to the right, so the blood wouldn't come out. My mom was on the left, I was in the middle, and I think someone was on the right. My mom had a washcloth on top of my head. It was so blurry and getting darker and darker on the way to the hospital. I remember shutting my eyes for a moment. Then, my mom shook me so I could wake up. My eyes kept opening, closing, opening, closing. I blacked out so many times I don't even remember who was driving (I think it was my dad). My mom was still holding me, trying to keep me awake. When we got to the hospital, my dad had to carry me & my mom was trying to keep me awake and my head up. So that I wouldn't' drip everywhere. They took me to the ER & saw me immediately. They laid me on a table & started to stitch me up. I don't even think they had enough time to numb it! If they did, it didn't work! My dad and especially my mom were crying. I mean I was their first born. But the doctors said I would be okay. I remember lying on the table, on my side, I couldn't see anything! They had to put a small, white sheet on my head.

That way the table wouldn't be covered with blood and it would be clean. They had to make a hole through the sheet so they could see what they were doing to me. I remember crying under the sheet because it hurt so badly. I had a really bad headache. I was in a lot of pain. I could feel the needle going in and out, in and out of my head. I wanted them to stop because it hurt. I wanted to get up and leave, it hurt so much. But, I knew it was for the best. I almost blacked out again. But, by the time I did, they were done. I wanted to go to sleep because it was late and I was tired. They wouldn't let me, of course. But, I was all right & now I'm here today with the scar of that painful night. I guess I had a guardian angel with me. I will never forget what my parents and the doctors did so I could be here today telling you this story.

However, I did not learn anything from that unfortunate incident. Whenever I can, I still jump on beds.

The Gift
2/14/02

His name was John. He was 6', with blonde hair and blue eyes. I'd say he was about 23 years old. He lived in a small New York apartment with his dog, Pepper. Pepper was a small lab. She was adopted from the shelter. Pepper wasn't a regular dog; she was sick. I guess that's why John got her. He could relate somehow.

For some reason, every time I walked by his apartment, I could see him in his bathroom window. He would stare in the mirror. He always looked angry and was always shouting! He never went to church, he never even came out of the house. I guess there's one of them in every neighborhood.

One day as I was walking down 9th Avenue, I noticed he was outside. I stopped by to see what he was doing, I was very surprised! He was "getting some fresh air" and smoking. I thought that was funny. He shouldn't be smoking in his condition. He never listened to me anyway. So, I just kept walking.

As I turned the corner, I noticed a little girl talking to him. It was Sarah, the neighborhood sweetheart. She was about eight years old and had long golden hair. She was one of those good girls. She always went to church and everybody loved her. Except John. Every time he saw her he made a terrible face. He never liked her. She was too happy.

"No one is that happy. Especially in this crazy world." He would always tell me.

I kept reminding him she was only a little girl and didn't know about the world and how crazy it was. He would just shrug it off and go inside, leaving me to feel like a dumb ass in front of his really small porch.

But, on this particular day, he didn't seem to have a problem with her. Obviously, he didn't know why. I could tell by the look on his face as she hugged him. Before she hugged him, they talked. I didn't know what it was about. I could not hear them. After the girl left, he went inside.

I followed him that night, as he was coming out his apartment. He went down this dark alley, in front of a fortuneteller shop. As he went in, I waited. I waited for about two hours before he finally came out. Whatever the gypsy told him must have been good. He had a sudden pep in his step. When he came out, he headed back to his apartment.

I figured I did enough eavesdropping for that night and went home. When I got there, I had a message on my machine. It was John! He wanted me to come over! I thought he saw me and was going to bust my chops for it. But, I went over anyway. I mean it couldn't be that bad.

As he opened the door to let me in, he had a huge smile on his face. It was freaky because he never smiled. I know. I'm his best friend. But, I've never seen him smile in the many years I've known him.

He has been smiling for ten years and will continue to smile until he's ready to leave this world. I've been by his side the whole time and I've been coming here every week. He would always think people would call him, "John the Cancer Patient". I told him he's full of it.

Author's Insight:

The second version of "The Gift". You decide which version you like better, if you like them at all. – I added the part about the gypsy fortuneteller because I've always had a thing for gypsies. Don't ask me why. I just find them fascinating. Also, for someone who is angry about his cancer, no faith, the feeling of nowhere to turn, even to his best friend. He (John) may need to seek council elsewhere.

Valentine
2/14/02

When we touch I quiver,

When we kiss I get weak.

When I'm with you,

I can do anything.

When I'm with you,

I'm free.

When we talk on the phone I get an extraordinary feeling

in my stomach,

When we are together no one else matters.

Right now, we are the only two people in the world,

Right now, we are engaged in a lover's embrace.

So this I will show,

I want to know.

Will you be my Valentine?

Author's Insight:

We were told to write a valentine poem, in my creative writing class. At the time, I did not feel I knew what the feeling of love was. I did not even think I had ever been in love before. But, obviously, I felt or understood something, because this is what I came up with.

The Secret to Life
02/25/02

A wooden frame
Three small squares
Polished to a shine
Windows

It holds
My whole life
With its rectangular shape
So full

With this
My life
Will be shared
From generation to generation

This frame
Is a diary
Ready
For the world to see

My Furry Friend
2/25/02

So small

Yet so cute

Crawling on the floor

All alone

His fur stands up

His tail is so fluffy

It twitches

He hears something

Perhaps a student

Nobody knows yet

All we know is that he's standing on his hind legs

So frightened

Yet so peaceful

All he has to eat are pecans

He has no problem with it

Just as long as he eats

And he has companions

Author's Insight:

My creative writing class was in the courtyard writing poems. I did not know what to write. I, literally, saw a squirrel not too far from me and came up with this.

Freedom Poem

3/4/02

Freedom is privacy

Freedom is music

Freedom is choices

Freedom is speech

Freedom is The Constitution

Freedom is Friends

Freedom is Family

Freedom is Civil Rights

Freedom is Writing

When I see the flag

I think of soaring

I feel I can fly

Let Freedom Ring!

3/18/02

Happiness is...

Schliterbahn

Rock concerts

Sleeping late after the concert the night before

Friends

Poetry

Back stage passes

The internet

Never having to say good bye

Loneliness is...

Saying good bye

Sunday mornings

No one who cares

No friends

No family

Knowing you didn't receive a Christmas card or Birthday

present

Sadness is...

A death in the family

No roses for Valentine's Day

An orphan

Moving away from loved ones

A broken chain

Kindness is...

Me

Hugs

Saying hi to strangers

Helping those in need

Fear is...

Being alone

Arguing

A dark alley

A 20 foot building

Being locked in a room

Never getting out

Death

Ashley

3/27/02

White face

Beautiful skin

Long brown hair

A friendly smile

Pouty lips

A beautiful mind

A caring heart

Big brown eyes

Did I just describe an angel?

Or is it a goddess?

Author's Insight:

My friend wanted me to write something about her. I stared at her for a bit, possibly making her blush, then wrote this…also making her blush.

Breaking Up
3/27/02

Correct me if I'm wrong,

But when you break up with someone you're not supposed

to get back together!

So then, why do people bother?!?

I know they "LOVE" each other,

But, who cares!

Nobody wants to hear,

"Yeah, we broke up again."

You would think it would be the end, right?

Wrong!

It's just the beginning,

In another week,

Maybe sooner.

You hear,

"Guess what!"

Then, that's when you know…

That's when you know,

It happened!

This is when you know,

That they got back together.

Then you wonder,

Why the hell did I agree to come over!

Does she ever shut up?

Yadda, yadda, yadda…

Time goes by,

Then, you realize.

You wonder,

You sit in your room and wonder.

You wonder if they broke up,

So, you wait.

Then, you get a phone call that will change your life

FOREVER!

It's your friend,

They broke up again.

At that moment you want to hang up.

But, you want to be a "good friend".

You stay on the line and listen,

You listen to her story while flipping the TV.

You act like you care,

But, you don't.

Deep down inside,

You could care less about her problems.

When you hang up,

You think if you should change your number.

But, being the good friend that you are,

You don't.

Instead, you sit in your room and wonder about next week.

Tale of a Teenage Bride
4/24/02

Something old: Mom's wedding dress
Something new: A baby
Something borrowed: Money
Something blue: Her hair

16
4/24/02

Pure,

Clean,

Clear.

White dresses,

Satin lace.

Young and restless,

A beautiful face.

Sometimes she cries,

Sometimes she doesn't.

She lies,

What would her parents do?

She has a bun in the oven.

She's only 16,

But looks 24.

If only he knew,

She's not that pure anymore.

7/19/02

I'm sick and tired of all this shit! People screaming, people bossing me around, people just fucking talking. Would they ever shut up? Why the fuck do I even care about their problems! I just wish they would all shut up and quit talking their shit! They need to understand a person could only take so much! A person gets annoyed after a while! I'm sick and tired of listening to all this shit! It sounds selfish, I know. But, you would be thinking the same thing too if all you ever did was listen! Sure, I'm a good friend, and a good listener, or so I hear. But, every now and then I wish people would listen to me for once! Everyone has problems, even me! I just need a friend that will actually listen to me instead of just ignoring me EVERY TIME I need someone to talk to! I just want a TRUE friend that won't backstab me and will treat me the way I treat them! This is why I write. Writing is my ONLY TRUE friend. It helps me escape.

Her name is _____ & her favorite color is green
8/2/02

Everything is so damn difficult. I can't even talk without everyone knowing about it. I can't even type without people bugging me or nosing around my business. Why won't people leave me alone? Why won't she leave me alone? I'm living with a psycho! Sometimes she is scary. Sometimes she freaks me out. She wants to know everything I do. She wants to know where I'm going. She wants to know who I'm talking to and why. She always wants to know what we talk about. I'm not even dating her and still she treats me like her exs. She's supposed to leave soon. But, now we're not sure. She gets jealous when certain people talk to me. She gets mad when people are nice to me. Why is that? What did I do to her? She envies me. But, I do not know why. I've always been there for her. I've always treated her right. I'm even a good listener and help her with her problems. If it weren't for my family she'd be on the streets right now. If it weren't for my family she would not be loved. I guess she realizes this and it makes her angry. She falls in love too easy and gets her heart broken fast. Everyone she's ever loved has been scared. Scared of what she might do. I guess I'm the same way because now I understand what they went through. Her name is _____ and her favorite color is green.

Why Kids Today are So Screwed Up
10/21/03

The earliest memory I have is when I was about six. I was jumping on the bed with my cousin and hit my head on a sharp edge of a wooden table. I had a gash on my head and was bleeding so bad I blacked out a few times. But, that's another story.

Parents

Another is when my brother, dad, and I were going to watch the Dallas Cowboys practice at St. Edward's University. It was during the summer and I was really hot. So, with my luck, I got sick. I don't know what happened. I think I got dehydrated. One minute I was having a good time; the next I was drinking ten small cups of water in the American Red Cross tent. I remember throwing up and feeling really bad. I had to stay in the tent for a while so I wouldn't pass out. We had to go home shortly after that, I had heat exhaustion. Then, I remember my dad yelling at me because we had to come back home. It wasn't my fault I got sick! It's not my fault it was hot! That is when I lost all respect for my dad...I was seven.

Bullies/Crushes

When I was about eight or nine, I was going to Galindo (fourth grade). I remember a lot of things that happened, surprisingly! One thing I remember is when there was a boy I liked and he thought I gave some girl his phone number. We kind of got into a fight. He pushed me against a wall and started yelling at me.

"Why did you give her my number?"

I thought this was funny because I didn't have his number to begin with. I started to yell back.

"I don't even have your number!"

He insisted that it had to be me who gave away his number. So, when he refused to let me go, I kicked him in the family jewels. He fell on the floor and started whining like a little baby. That's what he gets! The next day, he apologized to me. I'm not sure if we were friends afterwards. I don't remember.

Teachers

In second grade, we were taking a timed multiple choice test. I was on a roll. When the teacher told us to stop, I kept going. I didn't hear her! So, instead of taking points off my test or having a talk with me one-on-one, guess she felt she had to make an example of me, and ripped up my paper! It was so embarrassing. She told me that she was going to give me a zero. I'm in second grade people! I've never had a zero! So, I started to cry. She didn't say anything. She just kept teaching as if nothing happened. After school, I ran to my mom and told her what happened. She was furious! My mom was scheduled for a conference anyway. So, instead of going home, we had a little talk with Ms. Teacher. My mom told her good. I don't remember what she said. All I remember is that the teacher started crying and was turning red from embarrassment. It was perfect. The teacher was nice to me the rest of the year... I love my mom.

When I was in sixth grade, my mom came to my rescue again. I was in choir and we would have choir practice every day after school. One day, the teacher was having an off day or something, and my friends were goofing off and making me laugh. They were right next to me. What was I supposed to do? So, while the other kids are singing along and having a good time, we were laughing. I didn't think it was going to be a big deal because I was such a good student. I was WRONG! What does she do? She stops, looks at me, and singles me out in front of the whole class. This was much more embarrassing than the time in second grade. I was at an age where I actually cared what people thought. She told me that they should make a special school for people like me. I guess she was implying that I was slow and didn't know when to get serious. She was yelling at me for no reason! Sure, I was laughing. But, that was all I did. What about the others? They were the ones who were actually being bad. They were the ones who were loud. So, she sent me home, in tears. I left the room and went home. When I got to my house, my mom noticed I was crying. I told her what happened and how I felt. BIG MISTAKE! She was even madder than before. She called the office and asked for the teacher. Of course, she was not there. So, my mom told them what happened and to have her call right away. When the teacher finally called, I had been missing class for a while. Just until things got straightened out.

My mom had quite a discussion with the teacher. The teacher was apologizing because it was unprofessional for her to act the way she did. She was telling my mom that she had a wreck and was feeling bad that day. My mom was telling her that she was sorry she had a wreck. But, that was no excuse. She agreed. My mom was going off on her. Wouldn't you know it, she made that teacher cry too! How do I know all of this? I was standing right there and heard it all. Of course, when I finally went back to her class, I was her "favorite student". I wonder why...

Friends

When I was a freshman in high school, I call this my "goth era", I would wear a lot of black and dark make-up. I met my best friend. She seemed pretty cool and was into the same stuff I was. We hung out all the time and talked about everything. If I had known how she really was, I wouldn't have spoken to her at all.

Sure, we had some good times in high school and did a lot of things together, even smoked. We had fun. Then, I started to find out how she REALLY was. She was psycho! She was abusive and obsessive. I didn't actually realize it until she wouldn't let her boyfriends talk or look at other girls. Even if they were friends for a long time, she still wouldn't let them have female friends. Besides me, another friend, and her. Over time, she began not to like our other female friend and became obsessive over me! People swore we were going out! It was bad. We stopped being best friends about our junior year of high school. That is when her boyfriend got sick of her crap and started beating on her. They stopped for a while because of me. I don't know why I even helped out with that relationship. But, then they started beating on each other again. We didn't talk for a while. Well, not as much. We started being friends again our senior year. Notice how I say friends, and not best friends? Our relationship was damaged up to that point. We would hang out every now and then, more often than we did the year before, and go out to see local bands. After a while, the relationship started getting sour again and we parted ways.

A few months passed, she came to live with us for about three weeks. Man, what was I thinking? She WAS obsessed with me! I didn't really believe the rumors, until then. She did tell me before she had a crush on me. But, I thought she was over it. Anyway, she came to live with us for three weeks. She wanted to know what I was doing, who I was doing it with, where I was going, who my friends were – the list goes on and on. Like I said, people thought we were going out. At that point, I didn't really care for her as much because of what she did. So, when we got into arguments, I didn't care if she cried.

She's manipulative and cries for anything. I wasn't going to let her fool me like she did with everyone else. One morning I actually caught her staring at me, while I was asleep. That was it for me. I was freaking out the whole day. She was at work, so it was ok. When all of that was set and done, she went back home and we stopped being friends.

A year has gone by and now she is starting to contact me again. I don't know what to do. Sure, I'll talk to her. But, only as an acquaintance. I don't think I'll ever be her friend again.

Now, at the age of 19, I respect my dad a little better. I am going to college, volunteering, and looking for a second job. I have a lot of friends and people who actually care about me. My life has turned out pretty well.

Death of a Friend

11/04/07

You walk around high and mighty.

I can't help but wonder what you are thinking.

The fact is, we used to be friends.

But you did something I cannot forgive.

You betrayed me.

How could you?

You think I will forgive you.

It is not that easy.

I used to think we would be friends forever.

That nothing could come between us.

I almost thought you were my BEST friend.

How could I be so blind?

You fooled me.

It was pretty easy.

You've had practice.

I knew it.

I watched the whole thing.

It was funny watching you.

It was funny that you thought everything was going to be

ok.

But it won't.

It will never be.

For, tonight, you are dead to me.

Untitled
12/09/07

You saw me at a show,

I thought you liked me for me.

As the months went by,

I could not live without you.

I fell in love,

I thought you loved me too.

When I called,

You sounded so sincere.

When I told you I would be in town,

You wanted to meet.

I was so excited,

I left a pass backstage.

Only to find,

You never showed.

When I called to find out what happened,

There was no answer.

Days went by,

Still no call from you.

I thought we were meant to be,

I was in love,

Until I saw you at another show,

You were all over him.

Then it occurred,
You never liked me for me.

Author's Insight:

I wrote this in a blog, on MySpace. A few of you may know what I am talking about. In my years of street teaming and promoting, I have seen, and heard, a lot of things. The most common, are situations like this. There are many types of girls (and guys) who attend shows/concert/events. You have your fans (the ones who will pay for a show, just to see a performance), your groupies (who attend for one reason — which is sometimes needed on that lonely road), your band-aides/street teamers/promoters/etc (who attend for support — whether it is selling merch, spreading the word, or just showing they care), your gold-diggers (who attend in hopes of hitting it off with one of the band mates and they make it big; when the band is not doing well, they move on to someone else). The girl I wrote this about, I am not sure what "category" she would fit in. But, it could be a whole new type of person. What do you think?

Rap about Paper Plates
12/11/07

Yo yo, paper plates are cool. They keep ur floors clean. You
can eat pizza, bagels, or maybe even some greens.
You can put them in the microwave or even in the fridge.
But don't put them in the oven or they might singe.

Author's Insight:
Wrote this in the chat room of jonasbrothersfan.com

Family
01/08/88

Family can get you through anything,
Without family you have nothing.
Friends and lovers come and go,
But family will never put you down.
Words may be spoken,
Feelings might get hurt.
But in the end,
Your family will fix what is broken.
Even when you feel alone,
Like nobody can help you.
You know you can count on them,

You can always go home.
If you look,
You will find.
A slight peace of mind,
Because family is there till the end.
Even if you need a friend,
They will always understand.

Friends
01/08/88

Many people will say,
"I am your friend.
I will always be there,
Till the end."
But you do not know them,
How do you know?
Many people will say things to get close to you,
Especially, if they feel they will get something out of it.
Do not believe everything they say,
They will try to befriend you to get what they want.
They might do it to get a deal,
They might do it and make you think they are ill.
Either way,
Be careful.

There are a lot of selfish people in this world,
That will do whatever it takes.
And that's sad,
Sad but true.

REAL Friends
2/22/08

These are the people that were there since the beginning,
These are the people that were there through the good times,
and the bad.
These are the people that will support you, no matter what.
These are the people that will look out for you.
These are the people that will bring you soup when you are
sick.
These are the people that don't want to see you get hurt.
These are the people that still call you and care for you,
even though you have been a jerk.
These are the people that could care less what you look like,
how much money you make, what you wear, or if you're
popular.
These are the people that will be there, even when everyone
else isn't.
These people will be there till the end.
These people are your REAL friends.

Sell Outs
2/22/08

You call them sell outs,

Why?

Because they are doing something you are not,

They are living their dreams.

Sure they sell out,

Concerts.

They work hard,

And still manage to thank their fans any chance they get.

You call them sell outs,

Yet, you don't know them.

How can you tell them they are sell outs?

Do you even know what that means?

If anyone is a sell out,

It is you.

How can you sit there one minute praising them,

The next, dissing them.

You call them sell outs,

Why?

Can you answer me?

I will wait.

He Loves Me

3/5/08

He loves me she says.

He loves me.

That's all I hear.

He loves me.

Then what is that on your face?

He loves me.

She says.

She is so blind.

He loves me she says.

I love him.

We are meant to be.

He loves me she says.

Me and only me.

Then, why is he out so late?

He is at his friends.

He loves me she says.

He would never hurt me.

Then, what is that around your neck?

He loves me she says.

I can't hear you.

He loves me she says.

Do you want your juice?

He loves me she says.

Pull the tube from your throat.

He loves me she says.

I still love him.

Where is he?

He loves me she said.

She is not here anymore.

As I sit here.

Looking at her coffin.

I wonder why.

Why did she love him so?

Why did she always say he loved her?

I was about to ask,

When she stopped breathing...

Author's Insight:

Male or female, it is not right. The fact is, not everyone is lucky enough to get out while there is still time. My inspiration for this, believe it or not, was a song by Drake Bell called 'Somehow'. Once I heard that song, I fell in love with it. I started thinking of all the people I have known who have been in these violent situations. They know who they are, so there is no need to disclose this information. I wrote this in 2008, it was controversial then, and I am pretty sure it still is.

Death of a Friend
3/5/08

It happened a few years ago,

But I remember it like yesterday.

My dad picked me up from school,

It was a beautiful day.

But that is a day I will always dread,

That is the day I lost you.

I couldn't see much,

Everything happened so fast.

What I saw changed my life forever,

It is a day I will always remember.

I saw a car,

Maybe being chased.

The next thing I knew,

It collided into the back of a red pick up truck.

I could not believe what was happening,

It was so loud.

Glass everywhere,

People screaming.

Students passing by,

Wondering what was going on.

One of you I knew since 5th grade,

The other I knew from the halls.

I sat in the car in disbelief,

My dad got out and ran across the street.

Trying to help,

In any way he could.

Cell phones being used,

Everything going so crazy.

But still,

I sat there.

When the ambulance came,

I thought all of it was over.

I didn't know what I was about to see,

I didn't know this image would stay in my head for years.

Even now,

I can't believe it.

It turned out,

One of you left instantly.

They had to cover you,

Cover you from view.

I thought that was that,

They have done their job.

I didn't know about the weather,

I didn't know it would be windy that day.

When I turned to my left,

All I saw was you hunched over the steering wheel.

I turned my head the other way,

A tear running down my cheek.

I saw a friend out the window,

I looked up at him.

He seemed so sincere,

He couldn't believe what we have seen.

My dad came back in the car,

Telling me about the other boy.

He was hurt bad,

Bleeding from the ears.

He told me he talked to him,

My dad told him everything was going to be ok and he was

going to the hospital.

I had my head down,

Not believing a word I just heard.

He asked me what was wrong,

I said nothing.

The next day was sad.

The other boy left at the hospital.

We cried,

We all came together and cried.

We couldn't believe our friends were gone,

We couldn't believe we would never see them again.

I went home and told my dad who they were,

I knew them.

Then, he said that he was the last one that guy talked to
and saw.
Yeah, and I'll never see them again...

How I Really Feel
3/12/08

I almost cut myself today,

I was in the shower shaving.

Then I thought to myself,

What if I just end it all now?

I bet they wouldn't even care.

By the time they'd notice,

I'd be dead.

As I shave my legs,

I look at the blades.

Pondering these words,

Over and over.

I stand there and stare,

I stare at the blades.

I wonder what the blades will feel like,

I take my fingers and run them across the blades.

Nothing happens,

I don't have time.

I have to wash my hair,

I close my eyes.

I close my eyes and see my little sister,

What would she do without me?

What would I do if she were the one that found me?

Who would teach her things my mom can't?

What if they hate her as much as they hate me?

I couldn't deal with that.

As I get out of the shower and dry myself,

I am thankful I didn't.

It wasn't time for me to go,

Now, I have to go downstairs and face it all again.

5/__/08

She keeps saying that she will be ok,

Then why is she in the hospital almost every day?

She takes her medicine,

So she will not be sick.

She tells us everything will be fine,

I don't believe her.

When she told us what they found,

I was scared.

I didn't say much,

I need to be strong.

She tells us if she doesn't have surgery,

It can be fatal.

But how can she do this,

When she could die on the operating table.

She tells us she will be fine,

Everything is ok.

But I see,

I see her every day.

She is weak,

She can't do the things she used to do.

Being the oldest,

She tells me.

If anything happens,

I will be in charge of everything.

What am I supposed to say?

My heart weakens more & more each day.

You don't know how it is,

To watch someone you love.

So I sit here,

Waiting for the day.

The day she will either get better,

Or fade away.

Don't go mom,

I'm not ready.

My Island
1/21/09

At my island, there is an ice cream stand.

At my island, you can rest your hands.

At my island, you don't have to worry about how much

money you make.

At my island, no one is fake.

At my island, you are free.

At my island, there are endless possibilities.

At my island, you can go to a carnival.

At my island, we won't let you fall.

At my island, there is a day spa.

At my island, you can relax and escape from it all.

Passing Ships
7/1/11

Like ships in the night,

We pass by each other.

Lost,

Wandering.

We sit at home,

Wondering if our love will ever come.

Is it possible,

That it's not meant to be.

It's hard to tell,

Because I think about you constantly.

Guarded
7/18/11

Love, I may shy away

But, that is only because I am afraid

You see, love

My heart has been locked away, safe

These barriers have been put up for protection

You may be the one I have been waiting for

If you unlock this cage of mine

I may just give you all of me

If you push me away

My heart will continue to be guarded

You say I am the apple of your eye

Yet, there is nobody by my side

Oh, love, show me something real

Instead, I am alone

Confused about what to feel

A Warm Place

11/29/11

A warm place would be nice.

Sunglasses. Just sitting back.

Relaxing. No worries at all.

A place to be alone.

Even for a moment.

The ocean breeze in your face.

A place like that would be nice.

Made in the USA
Charleston, SC
05 June 2015